CONTENTS

KV-374-731

This picture shows the Kalsi family: Mrs. Kalsi, Mr. Kalsi, Inderpal and Inderjit. They are just coming out of their home. It is a ground floor flat. They live in the suburbs of Delhi, which is a large city in India. (Suburbs are the parts of a city away from the city centre.)

- Can you find India and Delhi on your classroom globe or on a world map?
- How many people are there in your family?
- Do a classroom survey on the size of families. How is the Kalsi family the same or different from families in your class?

- What do you think the ramp up the steps is for?

Families in India are often much bigger than the Kalsi family. They are often much bigger than families in Britain too.

Here is a family who all live together. They live in a large mud-brick, thatched house in a village near Delhi.

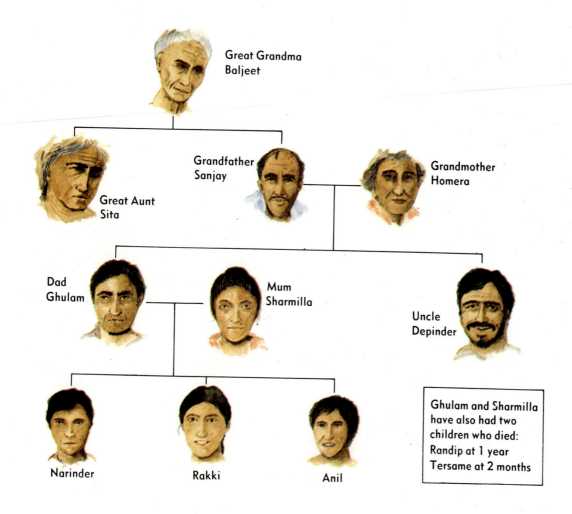

Great Grandma Baljeet

Great Aunt Sita

Grandfather Sanjay

Grandmother Homera

Dad Ghulam

Mum Sharmilla

Uncle Depinder

Narinder

Rakki

Anil

Ghulam and Sharmilla have also had two children who died: Randip at 1 year Tersame at 2 months

- How many people live in the same house?
- How is Ghulam and Sharmilla's family different from yours?
- Do you have a great grandma? Where does she live?
- Where do your grandparents live?
- Why might it be a good thing for a large family to live together like this?
- What problems might it lead to?

The drawing above is called a family tree.
- Try to draw a simple family tree yourself.

The Kalsi family are having a meal with their friends, the Chanas, in the living room.

- Where is Mrs. Kalsi? Where is the little girl, Baljeet?
- What do you think Mrs. Kalsi is doing?
- Where will she sit when she comes back?
- How are the people arranged around the table?
- Draw a plan to show where the women, the men and the boys are sitting. Describe where the fridge is.
- Make a list of all the furniture you can see in the room. Now make a list of the things found in your living room. How do the two lists compare?

Here is a plan of the Kalsis' living room. It is drawn as a fly on the ceiling might see it. Two pieces of furniture are missing.

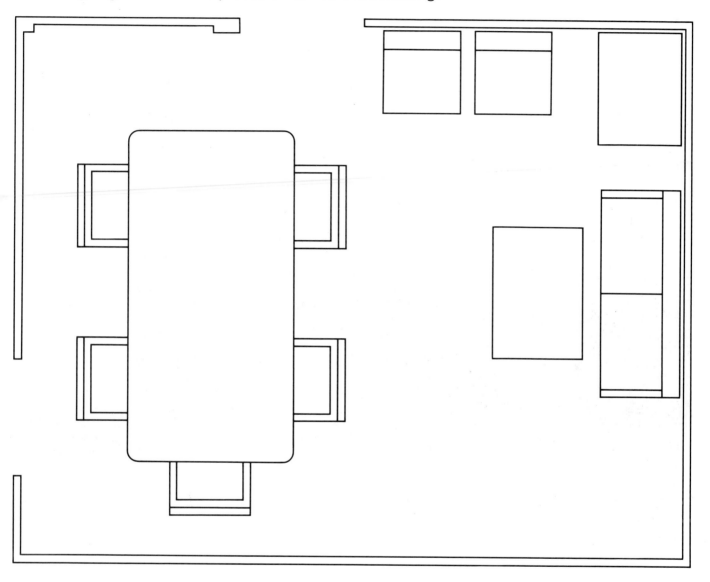

● Trace the plan and then:

■ add the two missing pieces of furniture.
■ label the dining table and the fridge.
■ mark where the boys are with green dots.
■ mark where the little girl is with a red dot.
■ mark where the adults are with blue dots.
■ show with an arrow where Mrs. Kalsi is.

Draw a plan of your own living room at home. Say how it is the same as or different from the Kalsis' room.

This picture shows the Kalsis' home and other homes nearby.
The family is just arriving home in a taxi with some friends.

- Draw the table below in your book. Fill it in to compare
  homes in your street with homes in this part of Delhi.

	Homes in my road/street	Homes in this part of Delhi
Type of home (semi, terrace, flat)		Flats
Built mainly of? (Brick, wood, concrete etc)		
Shape of the roofs		
Gardens		
How are the homes arranged (in straight lines, curves?)		

This shows a simple plan of the rooms in the Kalsis' flat.

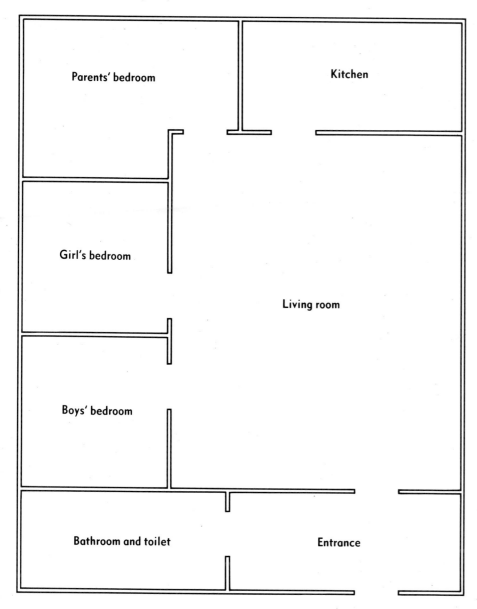

- How many rooms are there?
- Which is the biggest room? Which is the smallest one?
- Which two rooms are square?
- Which rooms are rectangles?
- Whose room is near to **a.** the kitchen **b.** the entrance
  c. the toilet?

- On a piece of tracing paper draw the plan of the Kalsis' flat.
  Then show the routes the boys would take around the flat
  as they get ready for school.

This is another home in India, near Delhi. In many ways it is quite different from the Kalsis' home.

- Look for clues to show:
  - that this home is in the country.
  - that it is a farm.
  - that it is quite hot.
  - that it sometimes rains heavily.
  - that it is near a main road.

There may be more than one clue to each thing.

In India people spend more time outside than we do but often need to be in the shade or to shelter from rain and sun. What have the people done here to provide themselves with shade and shelter?

Here is another home in India.

- How does it compare with:
  a. the Kalsis' home?
  b. the other homes on these two pages?
  c. your home?

Here is another house in the countryside near Delhi.

- Do you think it is newer or older than the house at the top of the last page? Say why.
- Describe the house and say how it is the same as and different from yours.
- Think about:
  - its size, height and shape.
  - its doors, windows and roof.
  - what it is made of.
  - the space around it.

The people are in a group or cluster.
- Where have they all collected?
- Why have they chosen to group together in that place?

Many people in India live as Indira does in the picture below.

> Indira's home is made of bits of wood, cardboard, tins and pieces of cloth. It is one room 3 metres by 4 metres. Inside there are only a few boxes.

- Compare Indira's home with the Kalsis' home (on pages 2-5) and with your home. Finish this table.

	Indira's home	The kalsis' home	My home
Number of rooms			
Size	Very small.		
Furniture			
What it's made of			
How it looks			

The people who live in these homes are a little better off than Indira. Their houses are made mainly of stone. This keeps the rain out but the rooms are small and overcrowded.

- Name three ways in which these homes are different from Indira's.
- Why do you think these houses will not get flooded when it rains heavily?
- Would you like to live here?

No homes

Many people in India have no homes at all. The family below lives, eats and sleeps on the pavement. They are in front of a shop.

- What will happen to them when the shopkeeper comes to open his shop?
- What must it be like to spend every night sleeping on the pavement?

- What problems will any of the people on these two pages have when:
  a. they want to make a meal?
  b. they want to have a wash?
  c. they want to go to bed?

- How do you think they will spend most of their time?

As in this country, there are local shops in the suburbs of Delhi. This shop is near the Kalsis' home.

Outside the shop

Shopping list

Rice
Soap
Peppers
Semolina
Potatoes
Eggs
Garlic
Sugar
Ginger
Talcum Powder
Cough mixture

- Can you see the steps (A), the chairs (B) and the shutters (C)?
- What do you think:
  a. the chair is for?
  b. the steps are for?
  c. the shutters are for?

Inside the shop

- Describe what the shop looks like outside and inside.
- Can you see things in the shop that you might buy in your local shop?
- What sort of shop is it? Which items on the shopping list will be bought here?
- Make two lists of the ways this shop is the same as and different from a shop near you that sells the same kind of things.

In Delhi there are open markets like the one on the left. They are open every day of the week. The markets give people a chance to sell some of the things they grow.

- Which things on the shopping list are likely to be sold here?
- What types of food are there?
- Have you visited a local market near you?
- What things are sold there? Can you think of two reasons why people buy in the local market rather than from shops?

One of these shops below is the last one which needs to be visited.
- What is left to be bought? In which shop will it be found? If you look carefully you will see that there is a doctor's surgery next door.
- Why is this a good place for a surgery?
- How does this parade of shops compare with one near you? Think about the appearance of the shops and the traffic.

THE HIGH STREET SHOPS

THE HIGH STREET SHOPS

If Mrs. Kalsi wants other things bought, it may be necessary to go to a larger shopping centre or even into the centre of Delhi. Here is a view of another parade of shops near the centre of Delhi.

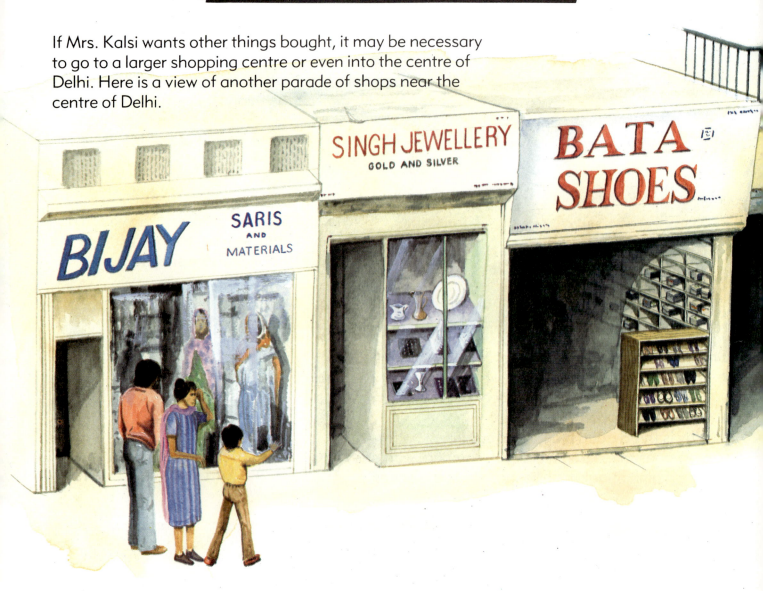

Here is the Kalsis' shopping list for a visit to the High Street on a Saturday morning.

- How many shops do they need to visit?
- Write out the list so that they can visit the shops in order.
- Which shop in the picture do they not visit?
- Which item on their list will they not be able to get from these shops?
- Make a list of things you can buy in each shop.
- The shops here all sell different things but in what ways are they the same?

Shopping list
Chair
Tennis racquet
Cotton for a blouse
Earrings
Saucepan
Sari
Paint for the door
Kettle
Material for shirt

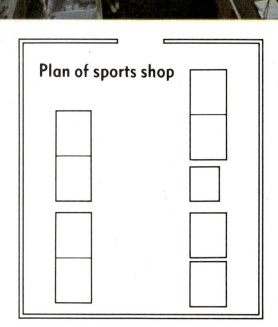

The family are in the sports shop. Like most shops it is really one big room for selling things. Everything is set out so that customers can choose and buy things easily.

- Trace the plan of the shop into your book and mark with coloured circles:
  - woman shop assistant (red)
  - 2 men shop assistants (blue)
  - 3 men customers (green)
  - woman customer (brown)
  - 1 boy customer (yellow)

Mark on your plan **a.** the door.   **b.** the large garden sunshade.   **c.** the balls on display.

Plan of sports shop

Here are the Kalsi family again, having a meal with their friends, the Chanas.

Let us see what they are eating.

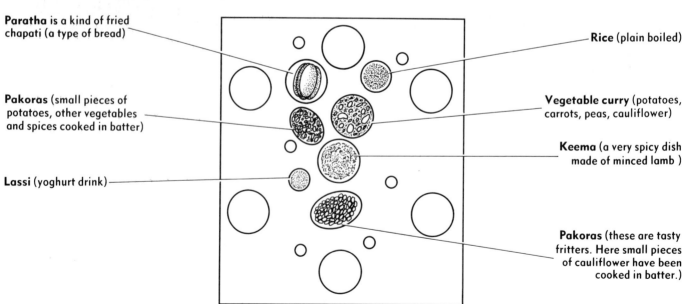

Paratha is a kind of fried chapati (a type of bread)

Pakoras (small pieces of potatoes, other vegetables and spices cooked in batter)

Lassi (yoghurt drink)

Rice (plain boiled)

Vegetable curry (potatoes, carrots, peas, cauliflower)

Keema (a very spicy dish made of minced lamb)

Pakoras (these are tasty fritters. Here small pieces of cauliflower have been cooked in batter.)

Afterwards they are going to have coconut barfi.

- Look at the foods on the table and make lists under these headings:
  Meat; Vegetables; Fruit; Salad.
- Indian food can be very spicy. Spices are vegetables which change the taste of food. Make a list of herbs and spices. Which ones do we use often? Can you find out where some of them come from?

- You could make two of the things that the Kalsis and the Chanas are having to eat. Here are the recipes:

Coconut Barfi	Lassi (Yoghurt drink)

Coconut Barfi

PREPARATION TIME: 20 minutes
COOKING TIME: 40-50 minutes

450g (1lb) desiccated coconut
450ml (¾ pint) evaporated milk
150-175g (5-6oz) sugar
225g (8oz) unsalted butter
8 green cardamoms, seeds removed and crushed

Dry roast coconut until pale brown. Remove from heat. In a non-stick saucepan, put the evaporated milk, coconut, sugar and butter. Cook on a gentle heat, constantly stirring the mixture, until oil separates 10-15 minutes.
Add crushed cardamom seeds. Cook until it is dry. Grease a flat dish. Pour mixture and flatten with a spatula dipped in cold water. Cook for 10 minutes and cut into squares or diamond shapes.

Lassi (Yoghurt drink)

PREPARATION TIME: 5-7 minutes

300ml (½ pint) natural yoghurt
50g (2oz) sugar
Pinch of salt
1 litre (1¾ pints) water
Pinch of saffron
10ml (2 tsp) lemon juice
Ice cubes

In a mixing bowl, beat the yoghurt well. Add sugar and salt, beat again and add water. Dissolve sugar by stirring well. Add saffron, lemon juice and ice cubes and serve.

We measure food by weight and in calories. You might know someone who is weight-watching. Weight-watchers add up the calories in the food they eat. If you eat too much food it is stored as fat. The amount of protein we eat is also important. Protein builds the body and keeps it in good repair.

What someone in Britain might eat in a day

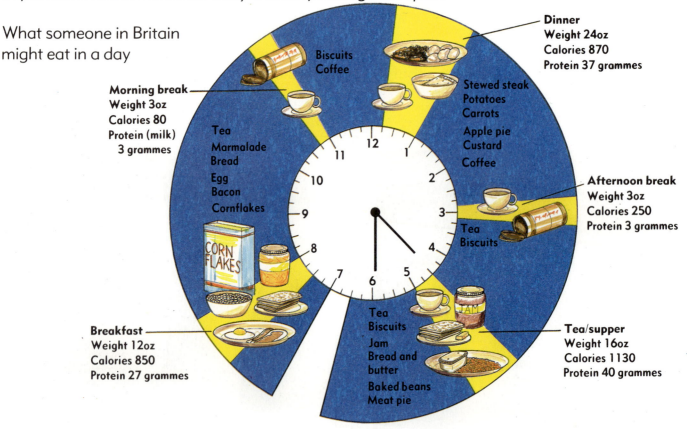

Dinner
Weight 24oz
Calories 870
Protein 37 grammes

Stewed steak
Potatoes
Carrots
Apple pie
Custard
Coffee

Biscuits
Coffee

Morning break
Weight 3oz
Calories 80
Protein (milk)
3 grammes

Tea
Marmalade
Bread
Egg
Bacon
Cornflakes

Afternoon break
Weight 3oz
Calories 250
Protein 3 grammes

Tea
Biscuits

Tea
Biscuits
Jam
Bread and butter
Baked beans
Meat pie

Breakfast
Weight 12oz
Calories 850
Protein 27 grammes

Tea/supper
Weight 16oz
Calories 1130
Protein 40 grammes

- Draw the table in your book. Fill it in from the clocks. Add up the columns.

	Britain			India		
	Weight (oz)	Calories	Protein (gr)	Weight (oz)	Calories	Protein (gr)
Breakfast	12 oz					
Dinner	24 oz					
Snacks	6 oz					
Tea / Supper	16 oz					
Total	58 oz					

The Kalsi family on page 2 are quite well off. On page 16 they are seen having a long meal with their friends. There are many people in India who have meals with their friends. During a day, many more people in India are likely to eat like this:

Lunch
Weight 16oz
Calories 540
Protein 19 grammes

What someone in India is likely to eat in a day

Rice
Onion
Carrots
Beans
Potatoes
Curd

Tea
Chapati
Plain
yoghurt

Buttermilk

Lentils
Carrots
Beans } curried
Potatoes
Rice

Breakfast
Weight 8oz
Calories 400
Protein 4 grammes

Supper
Weight 22oz
Calories 660
Protein 26 grammes

- Compare what people eat in Britain and India by drawing these graphs.

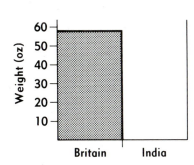
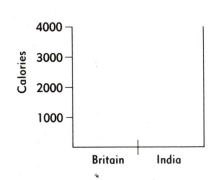
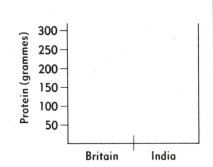

- Write down everything you ate yesterday and the day before. As the clock above shows, people in India often eat the same food at every meal and every day. Did you? Look at your lists.

This picture shows Mrs. Kalsi and Mrs. Chana in the kitchen. They are cooking. The food is cooked by gas.

- What vegetable is Mrs. Chana cutting up?
- Draw a plan of the workbench to show the cooker, three pans, a colander and two plates.

This picture shows chapatis being cooked in an Indian village. Chapatis are a kind of wholemeal bread. You can see balls of dough in the big pan in front of the bucket.

- What are the chapatis being cooked in?
- What fuel is being used to cook them?

When anything is made, **inputs** (or ingredients) are **processed** (made) into a finished object (or **output**). See how this works when making chapatis.

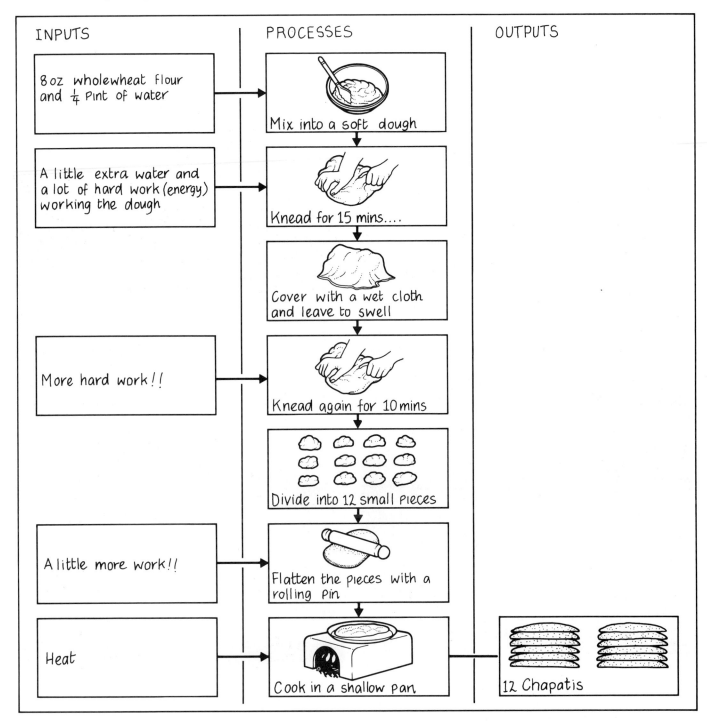

INPUTS	PROCESSES	OUTPUTS
8 oz wholewheat flour and $\frac{1}{4}$ Pint of water	Mix into a soft dough	
A little extra water and a lot of hard work (energy) working the dough	Knead for 15 mins....	
	Cover with a wet cloth and leave to swell	
More hard work !!	Knead again for 10 mins	
	Divide into 12 small pieces	
A little more work!!	Flatten the pieces with a rolling Pin	
Heat	Cook in a shallow pan	12 Chapatis

- Draw the 'story' of how something is made by your mother or father.

Mr. Kalsi is a civil engineer. His work takes him all over the countryside. His office is in Delhi.

On the right you can see him setting off for work. He often uses the bus. Sometimes he travels by tri-shaw or scooter-taxi. Do you know what a civil engineer does? He helps to make or build things like roads, bridges and dams.

Below you can see other people who make things.

- Describe what is happening in each picture.
- Which is taking place in a modern factory?
- Which of the views are the same as you might see in Britain?
- Which ones are very different? Say why.

This is a large factory in India. Many people work here.

In this factory the people make incense. India has many factories. It is a country with fast growing industries. These are usually found in the bigger towns like Delhi, Bombay, Calcutta and Madras.

- Describe what this factory looks like. (Think about its shape, size and appearance.)
- How does this compare to any factory near your school or that you have seen?

Find the industrial towns in your atlas or on the map on page 42.

AT WORK IN THE COUNTRY

Sometimes there is a small factory in one of the villages in the countryside. It is often a factory which makes things which can be used in that area. One such factory makes bricks.

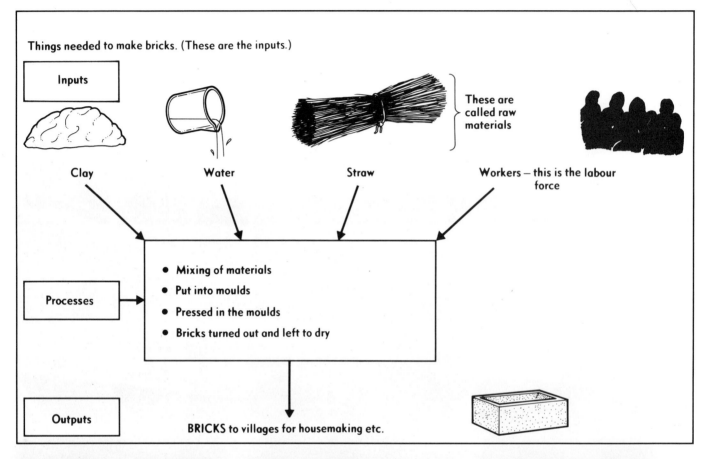

Things needed to make bricks. (These are the inputs.)

Inputs

Clay   Water   Straw   These are called raw materials   Workers – this is the labour force

Processes

- Mixing of materials
- Put into moulds
- Pressed in the moulds
- Bricks turned out and left to dry

Outputs

BRICKS to villages for housemaking etc.

- Describe:
  - how bricks are made.
  - how they are carried.
- Why do you think bricks are important to the village?

CRAFTSPEOPLE AT WORK

Skills in making things are often passed on from older to younger people. The things made by craftspeople usually need a lot of time, skill and care but not much machinery. A craftsperson usually does everything when making something. A factory worker only does part of a job.

- Here are some Indian craftspeople at work.
  - Describe what is happening in each picture.
  - For each picture draw a diagram like this and fill it in.

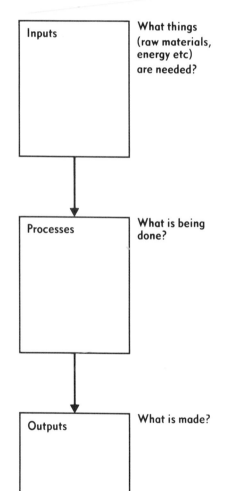

Inputs	What things (raw materials, energy etc) are needed?

↓

Processes	What is being done?

↓

Outputs	What is made?

Something to do in your classroom

Have a crafts exhibition. Collect from home examples or photographs of craftspeople's work. (Take care, the objects may be valuable.)

- See if you can find examples of these people's work:
  - potters, weavers, leatherworkers, basketmakers, wood carvers, blacksmiths, metalworkers.

- Can you think of any more to add to the collection?

As you have seen, in order to make things, raw materials are needed. Sometimes material which has already been used for something is used again to make something else. This is called **re-cycling**. You may have seen things like this:

Many people save bottles, paper and tins. These things go back to the factories and are re-used to make new glass, paper and metal objects.

One often sees things being re-cycled in India. Here are two examples.

- Write about what is happening in each strip.
  (*Remember: Inputs – Processes – Outputs!*)

Things to do

- Make a list of all the things in your classroom which have been recycled – made for one thing and now used for something else.
- Make something yourself out of waste cardboard, boxes, waste tins, waste cloth etc.
- Start collecting aluminium foil (from washed milk bottle tops and food trays), paper, tins and bottles. Find out where the nearest collecting places for these things are. Why are these good places for collecting bottles, tins and paper?
- Re-cycle paper by making a papier maché bowl or model.

Mrs. Kalsi is both a maker of things (in the kitchen) and a person who helps others. As well as looking after her family she also works for part of the day in her husband's office. She is a secretary.

- What does she do in her work?
- Describe the clothes she is wearing for work.

Here are some more helpers you might see if you walked down a street in Delhi.

- Describe what each one is doing.
- Do any of them have special clothes for their jobs?
- Which of them might you see if you walked down a street near you?

Many people in India are farmers. What they grow depends upon which part of India they live in. Around Delhi wheat, barley and millet are important crops. Here are some farming scenes.

The farmer in picture 1 is ploughing to break up the soil. Afterwards he will sow the seed. This is what his plough looks like.

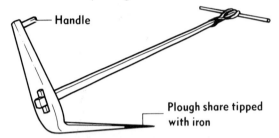

Handle

Plough share tipped with iron

- Describe how the plough is pulled through the soil.
- Describe the farmer's clothes.
- Make a model of the plough.

In picture 2 the crop is being harvested. It is being cut by hand with a long knife or sickle.
- Describe what is happening.
- Describe what the women are wearing.

After being cut, the stalks are tied into small bundles as shown in picture 3. Here a lot of bundles have been tied together to be taken back to the farm.
- Why do you think they are being carried like this?
- What else can you say about the women's dress?
- What does the dress tell you about the weather?
- Does all this look like easy work?

Not all farming in India is carried out by the methods shown above. Some farmers use modern methods and machinery.

In India children often have to work hard too.

Sometimes children help around the farm, as the girl on the right is doing. She is turning a machine which chops up food for cattle.

The boy on the left works all the time. He is very good at making clothes with his sewing machine. He works where passers-by can see him. They may ask him to make something for them.

The boy on the right works very hard with his donkey. They are carrying bricks from one place to another.

- Look at the pictures carefully.
- Which of the three jobs:
  - would you prefer? Say why.
  - looks hard and tiring? Say why.
  - do you think needs the most skill? Say why.
  - looks as though it could be quite dangerous? Say why.

In country areas in India almost all children walk to school. Some walk a long way. In the village on the left you can see a group of children walking through the village to school.

- How are the children dressed for school? What does this tell you about the weather? How can you tell that it is a sunny morning?
- Write sentences describing their walk along this street.
  Mention:
  - the road surface.
  - the buildings on either side.
  - people and animals.

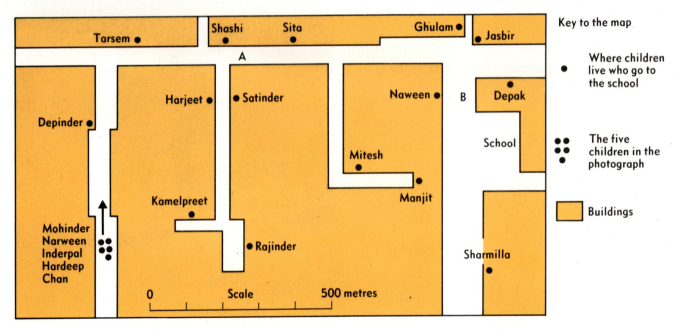

- This is a map of part of the village. Copy it into your book.
- Draw in the five children's route to school. How far do they have to walk?

- On your map neatly draw all the other children's routes to school.
- Who has the shortest journey to school?
- How far is Manjit from school "as the crow flies"?
- How far is it for her to walk?
- Who has a long and roundabout journey to school?
- Other children join the group on their way to school. How big will the group be at A? at B?
- Who will be going to school on her own?

These pictures show the village school and some of the boys at their lessons. The classrooms have open fronts but a screen can be let down if the weather is bad.

- Draw the school and write sentences saying what it looks like.
- How is it the same as and different from your school?

A lot of the school's activities and lessons take place outdoors. The boys in the picture are listening to their teacher who is outside the classroom.

- Why do you think classrooms are open and lessons take place outside?
- What are the boys using instead of books to write on?
- In what other ways is the classroom different from yours?

This picture shows some older girls in front of their school in Delhi. Many of the children will arrive by bus. Those who live close to the school will walk of course.

- Look at the school behind the girls. Write about the school saying something about:
  - how many floors it has.
  - how big it is.
  - what it looks like.
- Describe what two of the girls are wearing.
- What two clues suggest it is a bright sunny day?

These boys are at the school tuck shop.
- What are they doing?
- How are they dressed?

The inside of the school below is probably very like yours.

Many lessons are taken out of doors.
The children above are doing mathematics.
They use slates and chalk rather than boards.

On the right you can see how they are arranged for their mathematics lesson.

- How are the children arranged?
- How is your class arranged?
- Find Sanjay. He is in column C, row 5.
- Harjeet is in column _____, row _____ .
- Baljeet is in column _____, row _____.
- Where is Preetpal?
- Where is Shashir?
- When might the children be in groups or clusters?

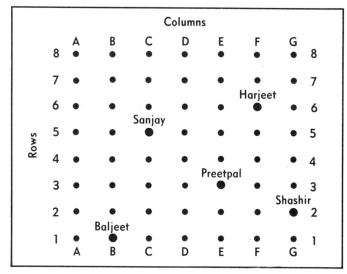

- What is happening in this picture?
- How are the children arranged?
- How is this school different from the one on the opposite page?

This picture shows Inderpal Kalsi having a shower. Modern homes in the towns have piped running water. Even here, though, water cannot be wasted. The water supply is often turned off for parts of the day to save it.

This picture shows women carrying water. Many families even in the large towns have to collect their water from wells and taps in the street. They may have to go quite a long way to get it.
- Would your mother enjoy fetching water like this?
- If she had to, she would expect you to be careful with the water you used. Make a list of ways of saving water so that the people in the picture would not have to make too many journeys in a day.

These village children are washing in the tank by a tube well. A hole has been sunk deep into the ground. A machine in the building behind the children pumps the water up to the surface. You can see how much water comes up. Washing like this seems to be fun.
- Would you enjoy it? Say why.
- What would the weather have to be like?

This graph on the right shows why water can be such a problem in Delhi. Delhi gets a lot of rain but it all comes at once.

- What is the driest month?
- What is the wettest month?
- How many months are dry?
- How many months are wet?
- Which months are very wet?
- Is it very wet in summer or winter?

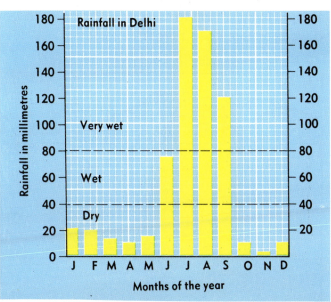

Rainfall in Delhi

Rainfall in millimetres

Very wet

Wet

Dry

J F M A M J J A S O N D

Months of the year

In town in the wet season

In the country in the dry season

Reservoir

Dam

Canal

Ditches in the fields
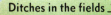

To try and make sure that there is water for crops all year, dams are built. These hold the water and let it out steadily. This picture shows one of the field ditches. Watering the land like this is called **irrigation**.

- What do you notice about the land in the picture?
- Trace the route of the water from the reservoir to the fields.

People living in villages near Delhi have to get their water from a well. This is how it works.

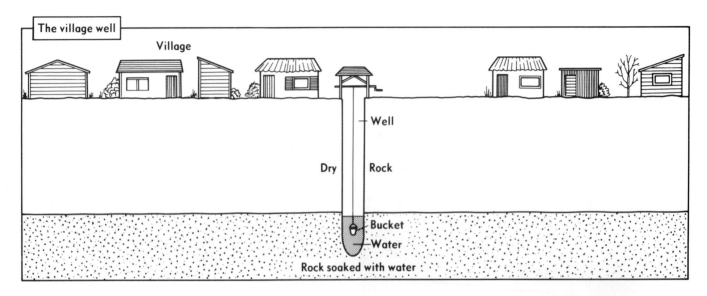

The well is dug until it reaches the rock soaked with water.
Water seeps into the bottom of the well. The bucket is lowered into the water. It fills and is pulled up.

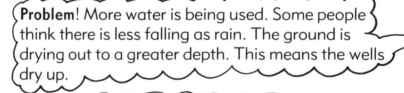

Remember! We each use about 120 litres of water a day. You just turn a tap for water. If you had to get it from a well you would be a lot more careful with it. You would use less!

Problem! More water is being used. Some people think there is less falling as rain. The ground is drying out to a greater depth. This means the wells dry up.

But they still need water in the villages.

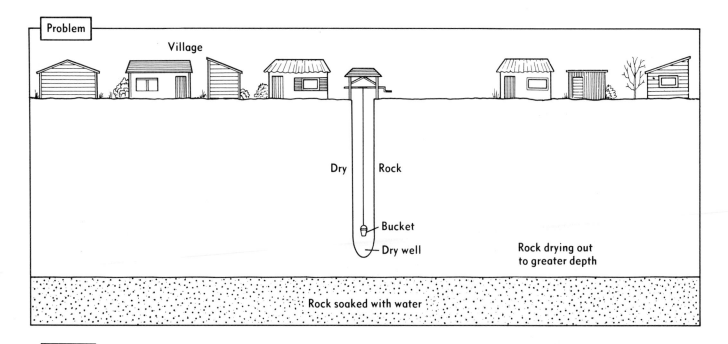

Problem

Village

Dry | Rock

Bucket

Dry well

Rock drying out
to greater depth

Rock soaked with water

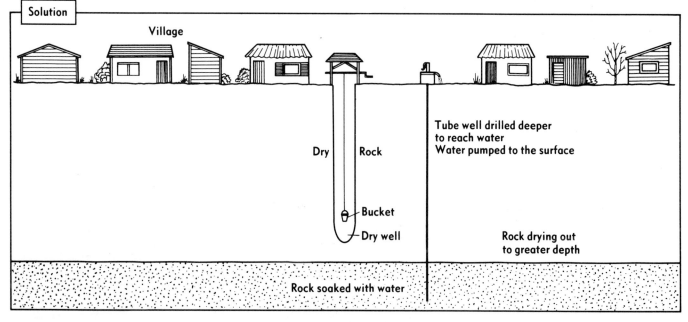

Solution

Village

Tube well drilled deeper
to reach water
Water pumped to the surface

Dry | Rock

Bucket

Dry well

Rock drying out
to greater depth

Rock soaked with water

- Write about how Indian villagers used to get their water.
  Some still do get their water like this.
- What must it be like in a village where the well dries up or
  takes a long time to fill with water?
- Think of all the ways you use water. How would your life be
  different if you were allowed only half a bucket of water
  each day for everything?
- What do you think might happen to the level of the water in
  the ground if a lot of tube wells are drilled?

This picture shows Mr. Kalsi and Inderpal setting off for the railway station. They are going to meet their friends, the Chanas. They are going by scooter-taxi.

- Have you seen a taxi like this before?
- How many wheels has the taxi got?
- How many people do you think it can carry?
- Why does it have no doors?
- How will the passengers be protected if it starts to rain?

This picture shows Mr. Kalsi and Inderpal on the station platform with their friends.

- What shows that the trains are well used in India?
- Are the carriages like those in Britain?
- What luggage have the Chanas brought with them?

Here they are outside the station. Some Indians believe that cows are holy animals. The cows are allowed to wander the streets. No one harms them.

- What kind of taxi can you see?
- How is the cow different from a cow in our country?

The Kalsis and the Chanas take a taxi home.
- Find the word NEW DELHI. This is the name of the station.
- What does the station look like? (Think about what it is made of, as well as its size, shape and decorations.)

The Kalsis and the Chanas pass along this road on their way home.

Picture search: how sharp are your eyes?
- How many different kinds of wheeled vehicles can you see?
- In how many different ways are people being moved? List them.
- In how many ways are goods being moved? List them.
- When something is moved, energy or power has to be used. What sorts of energy are being used in the picture? (Choose from this list: electricity, steam, oil or diesel, human, animal.)

- Choose words from these opposites to describe the street: busy/quiet; crowded/empty; quiet/noisy; warm/cold; clean/dirty; dangerous/safe; clear/blocked; exciting/dull.
- Can you think of any other words to describe the scene?

OTHER WAYS OF GETTING ABOUT

This picture shows two ways of getting about often seen in India.

- What are they? Which would you see in Britain?
- How do animals pull the cart?
- What is the cart made of? Do you think this is a quick way of moving things about?

Here are some more ways of getting about or carrying things sometimes seen in India.

Look at all the pictures on these two pages.
Make two lists under these headings:
- Ways of getting about found often in India and Britain.
- Ways of getting about found in India but not often in Britain.

GETTING ABOUT IN INDIA

India is a very big country. It would take you a very long time to travel across it by bicycle or bullock cart.

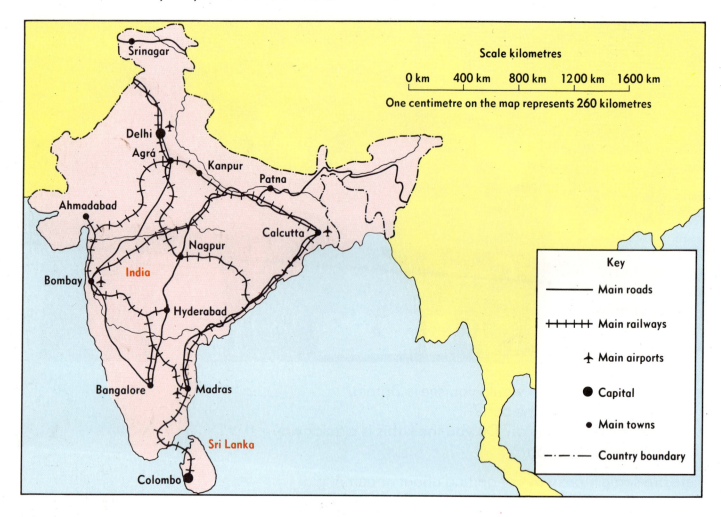

- How far is it 'as the crow flies' from Delhi:
  a. to Bangalore?
  b. to Madras?
  c. to Ahmadabad?
  d. to Srinagar?
- Find out how far it is from London to your home town.
- If you went by road from Bangalore to Patna which two towns would you pass through?
- How would you travel from Delhi:
  a. to Agra?
  b. to Nagpur?
  c. to Madras?
  Say why in each case.
- In which town do four railway lines meet?

For long distance movement in India aeroplanes, trains, buses and lorries are used.

Aeroplanes mainly carry people though they also carry mail and valuable goods.
- Where might you see a scene just like this in Britain?
- Can you think of any good reasons why aeroplanes move people rather than goods?
- Can you see planes from any other countries in the picture?

Trains carry people and goods.
- What type of engine is pulling the train?
- Would you see such an engine on a British main line? Why?
- Where might you see such an engine in Britain?

Lorries are used to move goods of all kinds. They usually travel shorter distances than the trains.
- Can you recognise any of the things on the lorries?
- Why are most of the goods well protected?
- Are the lorries like the ones you would see here? How are they the same? How are they different?

The two boys are playing Carrom. This is a favourite game in India. It is played on a Carrom board.

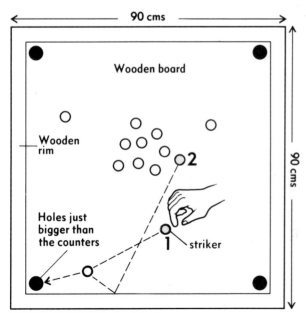

Here is a plan of the board.
The striker is used to knock the counters into the holes in the corners. If you knock one in, you get another go until you miss. Then your opponent can try to knock the counters in. You make the striker move across the board by flicking it with your first or second finger. The board has to be smooth and slippery. Talcum powder is good for this.

- Can you think of any of our games which are like Carrom? The drawing shows how one of the pieces was knocked in and where the striker stopped. Which piece would you go for now? Where might the striker stop after doing this?

Children play many of the same games all over the world. They like to play such things as mums and dads, catch, dares, pretend fighting, 'goodies and baddies', skipping games and ball games.

- Write about each picture.
  - What is being played or done?
  - What clothes are they wearing?
  - What does the weather look like?
  - What does the park look like?
Do you play or do these things?

- Describe your favourite game. Do you think it might be played in India?
- You could start a project on games played in playgrounds in different countries.

Can you find out?
India won the World One Day Cricket Championship in _____.
India were World Hockey Champions from _____ to _____.

A favourite outing for Indian families is a trip to the cinema.
Thousands of people go to the cinema once or twice a week.

- What is happening in the picture?
- Write down the names of three of the film stars.
- How does the cinema try to attract people in to watch the film?

Sometimes families will go to a café or ice-cream parlour before or after a visit to the cinema.
In this picture you can see the Kalsis and their friends in a café.

- Write about the scene in the café. Describe the room and the people.

Here is something else the two families did on their day out.

- Where are they now?
- Have you ever ridden on something like this? Why is Mr. Kalsi holding the rail? What do you think is going to happen?

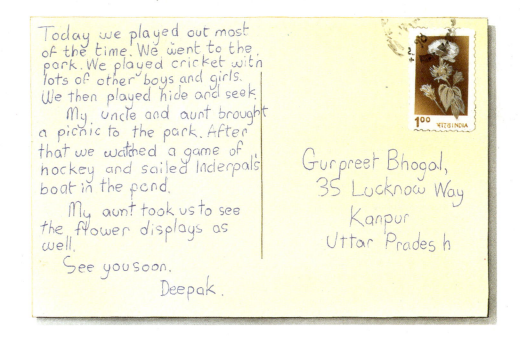

Today we played out most of the time. We went to the park. We played cricket with lots of other boys and girls. We then played hide and seek.

My uncle and aunt brought a picnic to the park. After that we watched a game of hockey and sailed Inderpal's boat in the pond.

My aunt took us to see the flower displays as well.

See you soon.

Deepak.

Gurpreet Bhogal,
35 Lucknow Way
Kanpur
Uttar Pradesh

Deepak Chana has written the postcard to his friend Gurpreet.
- List all the things they did in the park. Are they the sort of things you might do?
- The postcard is going to Kanpur. Find Kanpur on the map on page 42.
- How far is Kanpur from Delhi? What does the stamp show?

Page	Resources	Skills	Ideas	Follow up
2-3	Photograph Family tree	• Observation • Data collection • Classifying • Use of atlas	• Similarity/ difference • Views • Clues	Class survey of family size and composition. Research into and drawing up of family trees.
4-5	Photograph of living room Plan of living room	• Observation • Matching photo to plan • Plan drawing (room) • Classifying/comparing	• Distribution • Location	Drawing plans of bedroom, living room, classroom. Arranging given set of furniture in chosen room (in plan).
6-7	Photograph of houses House plan	• Observation • Classifying • Drawing a plan • Tabulating information	• Similarity/ difference • Pattern • Location • Movement	List and draw characteristic features of homes in school neighbourhood. Draw floor plans in children's own homes. Plot movements around classroom/school.
8-9	Photographs (of houses)	• Observation/comparison • Description	• Similarity/ difference • Clues/ evidence	Find out how houses differ in other parts of this country in terms of shape, size, building materials, etc. Try to explain the differences. Find out about other houses and homes in India.
10-11	Photographs (of houses)	• Observation/comparison • Tabulating information • Empathy	• Similarity/ difference • Clues/ evidence	Account for features of houses in school neighbourhood – e.g. sloping roofs, gutters, brick built etc. Mark out size of Indira's home in classroom.
12-13	Photographs (of shops, market, street)	• Observation/comparison • Description • Problem solving	• Clues/ evidence • Sequence • Best place/ location • Similarity/ difference	Visit local shops. Find out: what they sell, how they are arranged (plan), where customers come from.
14-15	Photographs (street scenes, shop interior) Plan (of shop)	• Classifying/listing • Problem solving • Tracing a plan • Using a plan	• Clues/ evidence • Sequence • Similarity/ difference • Location	Children find out what parents buy at local shops, surburban shopping centre (large), city centre shops.
16-17	Photograph Plan Recipes	• Relating photograph to plan • Classifying • Cooking	• Location • Similarity/ difference	Try recipes from other countries. Invite someone in from ethnic minority groups to talk about, help with, cooking. Find out what Indian foods the class likes and where the nearest Indian food shops and take-away are.
18-19	Clock/charts/daily meals in Britain and India Histograms	• Tabulating information • Comparison • Drawing graphs • Collecting information	• Similarity/ difference • Sequence	Find out other typical daily meals for other areas: African, West Indian, North American. Make a display of common foods from other lands.
20-21	Photographs Sequence charts (pictorial)	• Observation • Drawing a plan • Interpreting pictures	• Location • Process • Change • System	Draw a sequence chart of a favourite food being mde and cooked – plum pudding, fish fingers. What are the inputs, processes and outputs?
22-23	Photographs	• Observation • Classifying • Description • Atlas work	• Similarity/ difference • Process • Systems	Class survey of work done by fathers, mothers, elder brothers and sisters. Distinguish between people who grow things, make things (manufacturers) and people who help us (service industries).